LEARNING BASIC SKILLS THROUGH DANCE

FOR KINDERGARTEN THROUGH PRIMARY GRADES

LEARNING BASIC SKILLS THROUGH DANCE

FOR KINDERGARTEN THROUGH PRIMARY GRADES

**A Handbook of Motivating Activities
(Rhythms, Songs, Dances) for Developing
Motor Growth, Rhythm and Listening Skills**

by JEANNETTE LECAPTAIN

Publishers
T. S. DENISON & COMPANY, INC.
Minneapolis

 T. S. DENISON & COMPANY, INC.

Standard Book Number: 513-01207-9
Library of Congress Card Number: 72-77292
Printed in the United States of America
by The Brings Press
Copyright © MCMLXXII by T. S. Denison & Co., Inc.
Minneapolis, Minn. 55437

Foreword

Among educators, and especially physical educators, there is increasing concern for teaching children at an earlier age to use their bodies. Deficiencies are apparent at an early age. *Learning Basic Skills Through Dance* is designed to help the child with "slowed motor development." In elementary grades, attitudes are formed, and very often the poor performer is already feeling left out of things.

With specially designed exercises and activities, the early learner can master basic movements and apply them to a wide variety of motor skills he will encounter through his school years. In turn, we will free them of their fears of position change and height, giving them the balance and body control that will establish a feeling of physical security.

Specific sequential levels of learning are established in this series of rhythm and dance. Faulty movement is quickly "pinpointed" at the source of the problem. By learning the "part" before the "whole," children are able to experience success at many levels of performance, thus encouraging further physical effort. Motor learning, like any other form of learning, should be in gradual steps, forming the prerequisities for more intricate forms of movement.

All of the dance activities are preceded by a practice phrase which has the same movement reinforced in the dance itself. Rhythm and listening skills are enhanced through strong, easy-to-detect rhythm patterns. Suggestions are given for building further skills and associating these basic movements with folk and other dance steps.

Suggestions and diagrams for costuming that can be made in the classroom are given for each dance. You will find they are simple to make and inexpensive yet effective enough to use in a school assembly program.

CONTENTS

CLAPPING

Clapping is an elementary form of rhythm-making that can easily be performed by young learners. The easy to detect clapping pattern will give confidence to the child who may be reluctant to take that "first step." This clapping activity has a "cha cha" rhythm — slow, slow, quick-quick-quick and several intermittent counts of rest. These are all rhythm patterns they will enjoy and will be able to perform with ability. The small child will at the same time develop listening skills in order to perform rhythmically.

Clapping directions. Have the class sit in a large circle. There are two slow claps on the first measure of music, and three fast claps on the second measure of music. This rhythm pattern continues for the next four measures of music. On the seventh measure there is one clap followed by seven rest counts. The entire arrangement will be based on this pattern except on the last measure of music. Give the children complete freedom on this last measure allowing them to clap as many times as they wish.

Words can be introduced as soon as children are familiar with the rhythm pattern. It will add interest if the class sings the first sixteen measures and the teacher answers them on the last eight, preparing them for the final fast clap ending.

Building further skills. You can use this same music for building further motor skills. Have the children stand in a large circle, letting them jump in place using the same rhythm patterns they used in the clapping activity. Again use this same music and rhythm pattern performing alternating stamps in place. Have the class make combinations of clapping, jumping and stamping. Play with soft and loud combinations.

SIDE SKIP

Side skipping (chassé) is like galloping only it is performed sideways rather than progressing forward. Side skipping is the prerequisite for many physical activities during childhood years. Its transfer value can be seen in childhood games, folk dance, and even as a movement needed on the basketball floor. One side skip is a basic two step, preceded by a hop turns it into a basic polka step. The practice phrase below is used for children's first attempts at side skipping. Small children do not find it difficult to learn, however the teacher will need to stress the importance of stopping on the seventh count in order to reverse the movement.

Side Skip directions. Arrange the children in one or two well-spaced lines depending on the size of the class. Side skip to the right side for seven counts of music. On the eighth count rest in place with weight on the right foot. Reverse side skipping and rest on the left foot during eight more counts of music. Continue repeating for as many times as you wish.

CLAPPING

When we clap our hands, we must keep in mind

that we of-ten times stop!

Now we start a-gain, but re-mem-ber when

we might stop a-gain, stop!

That was ver-y good, now we wish you would

clap your hands real fast, now!

(clap) etc

SIDE SKIP

moderately

David Laakso

HALLOWEEN GHOST DANCE

Early motor skills of walking, jumping and side skipping are used in the Halloween Ghost Dance. The dance begins with the children standing in place in a well-spaced straight line. If class is large use two lines. Hold these positions during the two measure introduction.

STEP ONE

A. Side skip to the right side for seven counts of music. On the eighth count rest in place with weight on the right foot. Reverse side skipping and rest on the left foot during eight more counts of music.

B. Jump backwards (1 count), rest (1 count), jump backwards (1 count), rest (1 count). Using a quicker tempo jump backwards three times (3 counts) and rest (1 count).

C. Lift arms up and down in ghostly manner at sides of body (8 counts).

STEP TWO

A. Starting on the right foot take four scary, sneaky walks forward using two beats of music for each walk step (8 counts).

B. Repeat part B from Step One (8 counts).

C. Repeat all of Step Two again (16 counts).

STEP THREE

A. Repeat all of Step One (32 counts).

ENDING

Starting on the right foot, take two scary, sneaky walks forward using two beats of music for each step. On last two measures of music, take three big jumps and yell a big loud BOO on each jump.

Halloween costuming suggestions on page 42.

HALLOWEEN GHOST DANCE

David Laakso

STEP - HOP

Step-hop is a very important stage of motor development in early childhood. When a small child learns to step-hop they have achieved the necessary skills for skipping. If you are working with very young children, your first concern should be whether a child can hop on each foot individually. Small children are inclined to hop on their dominant foot as this is the easiest and natural side. When the need to change feet is pointed out to them they will make the effort to alternate. For some it will be a completely new experience if their early years have been somewhat restricted and limited in activity.

Playing a game of "hobble hop" is a good pre-activity before small children attempt to step-hop. To play "hobble hop" you stand on your right foot and flex the left knee so that the left foot can be held with the left hand. The "stunt" is to hop around a few times on the right foot in this position. Then hobble hopping is performed in the same manner on the left foot. For very small children this game has challenge and "stunt appeal" which they enjoy.

It will help understanding if step-hop is demonstrated and practiced the first few times without music. Children will be less anxious and willing to listen to instructions. The easiest procedure is to learn step-hop in place without progressing forward.

<u>Step-Hop directions</u>. Start this movement by having the right foot off the floor. Step on the right foot, then hop on the right foot. Step on the left foot, then hop on the left foot. Continue on alternating till the end of music. As soon as children learn to step-hop in place allow them to progress forward when they perform this movement. To make a natural transition into skipping increase the tempo slightly as they step-hop forward.

STEP-HOP

David Laakso

THANKSGIVING SONG AND DANCE

This is a song and dance that can be used for your school program or for a holiday activity in the classroom. Select a child for the Indian chief, Pilgrim woman and Pilgrim man. The remainder of the class will be Indian boys and girls. Change "leads" from time to time to give other children a chance to be singled out.

Song and Dance directions. Arrange the class in a semi-circle as illustrated with arms folded and legs crossed Indian fashion. Sing the song once through in this formation before you begin the dance.

DANCE
(no movement on introduction)

STEP ONE

Bring both arms overhead and open them to the sides in a big circle (2 measures). Fold arms in front of chest 'Indian fashion' (2 measures).

REPEAT ALL of Step One only start rising when you fold arms in front of chest the second time (4 measures).

STEP TWO

Do four step-hops alternating, starting with the right foot and progressing forward in a single clock-wise circle (2 measures). Next shuffle forward with tiny steps with arms folded in front of chest (2 measures).

REPEAT ALL of Step Two (4 measures).

THANKSGIVING

Lillian Lindley

David Laakso

INTERLUDE

The Indian chief and two Pilgrims walk to the center of the dance area. The remaining Indian boys and girls form a large circle around the three "leads," kneeling down on the floor and sitting back on their feet.

STEP THREE

Pilgrims and Indian chief pretend to smoke peace pipe. At the same time the Indian boys and girls resume the song and do the following: raise both arms overhead, tip bodies forward and sweep both arms down and behind body with palms up (2 measures). Return arms (lifting body) back to overhead position (2 measures). REPEAT ALL of Step Three. (4 measures).

TAG ENDING

Indians on floor return arms to folded position in front of chest. Pilgrims and chief place one arm forward touching each other's fingers in a gesture of friendship.

HEEL-STEP

This heel-step dance step is used in many folk and square dances. It is also used as a basic step in the "Toyshop" production that follows. Practice on this step will also allow children to perform a kick-step or toe-step as they are fundamentally the same. Use the practice phrase below for heel-step practice.

<u>Heel-step directions</u>. With leg straight, touch the right heel forward with toe turned up (no weight); then step on the right foot in place. With leg straight, touch the left heel forward with toe turned up (no weight); then step on the left foot in place. Continue alternating for practice.

David Laakso

Thanksgiving costuming suggestions on page 43.

CHRISTMAS TOYSHOP DANCE

This "Christmas Toyshop Dance" is an outstanding stage presentation that has real appeal to the audience as well as the performers. There is special excitement for young learners as toy movements are something they can understand and interpret through movement. The story action will be clear and easy to follow.

Information before starting the dance. There is one toymaker. The rest of the class are either toy soldiers or dolls. For the toymakers part you will need a hammer, large key (made of cardboard) and a toy bugle or similar instrument. A small chair or other such item can be used as the toy being built by the toymaker. When children first learn the dance, the toymaker's part should be played by the teacher.

The toy soldiers and dolls perform with a stiff mechanical movement. Dolls' arms are held at the sides of their body with elbows bent and fingers stiff; toy soldiers' arms are held close to the sides of their bodies with elbows bent to form right angles. These stiff arm movements are held through the dance. The body movements are also stiff and "toylike." This "toylike" movement can be demonstrated to the class by showing them a wind-up toy in action. It is performed by keeping the legs stiff while moving with tiny little shuffle steps on the whole flat of the foot.

Music note. Play the music through for the children letting them hear the action. The music is written in 2/4 timing. It will be easy for children to understand if a measure is counted 1 2 3 4 rather than 1&2&.

Arrange the class as diagrammed to begin the dance.

DANCE DIRECTIONS FOR TOYSHOP

<u>Introduction (played by toymaker)</u>. Hammer on a toy prop such as small chair, rocking horse or such (2 measures).

Quickly scurry over to toy soldiers and dolls pretending to fix a sagging arm or tilted head (2 measures).

Move quickly behind the row of soldiers pretending to wind each one up individually. There are four measures of music for winding up toys. These same four measures of music can be repeated for as many times as you wish (depending on how many toys are to be wound up). It will be effective if each toy gives a slight jerk as the key touches its back.

On the last two measures of introduction the toys' hands are quivering jerkily at sides of body as if all wound-up and ready to go.

SOLDIERS ONLY
(Dolls hold pose)

STEP ONE

A. Heel-step with the right foot then heel-step with the left foot (1 measure 1 & 2 & – easier to understand counted 1 2 3 4). Starting on the right foot march four times in place alternating (1 measure).

REPEAT ALL of A two more times (4 measures).

B. Turn once around to right in place with "toylike" movement of feet (2 measures).

STEP TWO

A. Soldiers REPEAT ALL of Step One again (8 measures).

OFF-KEY BUGLE BLOWS
(Toymaker blows bugle)

As the toymaker blows his bugle, the soldiers and dolls exchange lines. This is done by using a "toylike" movement of the feet. The soldiers move backwards cutting through the doll line at the same time the dolls are moving forward (3 measures). Soldiers continue to face forward as they move back.

Dolls are now in place ready to perform while soldiers hold their pose in back line. Note diagram of line movement on bugle blow.

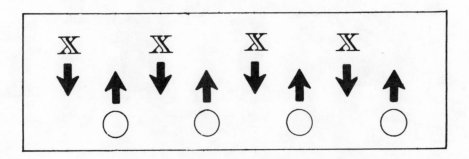

DOLLS ONLY
(Soldiers hold pose)

STEP ONE

A.   Heel-step with the right foot then heel-step with the left foot (1 measure). Make one turn to the right in place with a "toylike" movement of feet (1 measure).

REPEAT ALL of A two more times (4 measures).

B.   With jerky quivering hands slowly lower them at sides to waist level and bring them back up to original position (2 measures). Palms of hands continue to face front on this movement.

STEP TWO

A.   REPEAT ALL of Step One again (8 measures).

OFF-KEY BUGLE BLOWS
(Toymaker blows bugle)

Dolls and soldiers exchange lines back to original opening lineup, using the same movement as last bugle blow (2 measures).

SOLDIERS AND DOLLS
(All dance together)

STEP ONE

A.   Strike the right heel forward on the floor three times in succession (no wt.), step the right foot back in place (1 measure). Strike the left heel forward on the floor three times in succession, step the left foot back in place (1 measure).

B.   Heel-step with the right foot then heel-step with the left foot (1 measure). Make one turn to the right in place with a "toylike" movement of feet (1 measure).

REPEAT ALL of Step One three more times (12 measures).

STEP TWO
(Toymaker directs toys to do following action)

A.   Dolls turn to face right side wall and progress forward into a tightly closed single file line using a "toylike" movement with the feet. At this same time soldiers are forming their single file tight line moving to left side wall (4 measures).

B.   Toymaker gets in back of doll line and pushes them off side exit. If dolls use the proper "toylike" movement it will appear as if the toymaker is pushing the dolls off mechanically.   At this same time the soldiers have turned to the front and have slowly unwound. They have done this by slowly dropping down to a stooping position with most of the weight on their left foot. B takes two measures of music. The soldiers must be in a tightly closed line in this stooping position in order to complete the surprise ending which follows.

ENDING

The toymaker blows his bugle and the soldiers do not move (2 measures). He takes one look at them questioningly, then pushes the first soldier. This push has a chain reaction. One soldier after the other falls over to the floor in a follow-up manner right down the line. With a shrug of the shoulders, the toymaker takes his bow.

TOYSHOP

David Laakso

Christmas Toyshop costuming suggestions on page 45.

TURNS TO RIGHT AND LEFT

For the first time in this series left turning is introduced and will be used in the dance that follows called "Edgar (Snowman) and His Copycats." Turning to the right is the most natural way for most children to turn. A small percentage (usually left handers) will have a natural inclination toward left turning. Through practice, children will experience a kinesthetic feel and learn the difference between a right and left turn. Use the practice phrase below for practicing these turns.

Turns Right and Left. Turns are done by taking a series of small steps on the balls of feet. Turn slowly in place to the right coming to a full stop on the fourth measure. Repeat this same turn reversing to the left. Continue alternating turns for practice.

David Laakso

EDGAR AND HIS COPYCATS
(SNOWMAN)

This is a song and dance that can be used as a "showy" stage performance or as a "fun" activity in the classroom. Select one child to be the snowman. The remainder of the class are copycats. On the first verse the copycats sing to the snowman as they pretend to build up his body with snow. The snowman then begins to dance with the copycats imitating his movements. Following the dance the second verse is sung while the class joins together in a long train line and pushes the snowman off. The class members should have turns in playing the part of the snowman but in the beginning a child with ability should be selected.

23

SONG AND DANCE DIRECTIONS
(Snowman is alone in dance area)

Introduction. The class gathers around the snowman (4 measures).

Lyrics. Copycats sing the first verse of the song while at the same time pretending to build a snowman (8 measures).

Interlude. The snowman moves forward. At the same time the copycats form one or two well-spaced lines behind the snowman ready to start the dance (2 measures).

STEP ONE
(requires 8 measures of music)

A. Snowman (SM) steps on right foot and hops three times on right foot (1st measure). Copycats (CC) repeat same (2nd measure). SM steps on left foot and hops three times on left foot (3rd measure). CC repeat same (4th measure).

B. SM turns to right in place with tiny mechanical steps on balls of feet (5th measure). CC repeat same (6th measure). SM turns to left in place with tiny mechanical steps on balls of feet (7th measure). CC repeat same (8th measure).

STEP TWO
(requires 8 measures of music)

A. SM moves forward with tiny mechanical steps on balls of feet (9th measure). CC repeat same (10th measure).

B. On the 11th measure of music the SM makes a big jump landing with feet apart (2 beats) then CC repeat jump (2 beats). On the 12th measure of music the SM and the CC all jump in unison three times.

C. Repeat all of A and B of Step Two only move backwards on the mechanical steps (4 measures).

STEP THREE
A. REPEAT ALL of Step One (8 measures).

LYRICS

Sing the second verse of the song. At the same time start forming a joined train line behind the snowman (4 measures). Push the snowman off while slowly moving in a "choo choo" train line and waving good-bye (4 measures).

TAG ENDING

Run back to seats or off stage if used for a performance.

Costuming suggestions for this dance on page 48.

24

EDGAR and HIS COPYCATS
(SNOWMAN)

Moderato

David Laakso

Ed-gar is the snow-man, we made of ice and snow,

see him dance so round and fat, we are all his co-py-cats.

Ed-gar is the snow-man, we made of ice and

snow, the sun is high, we'll wave good-by as off he has to go.

JIGGING
(coupé)

Jigging is a motor skill that requires quicker and finer movements. It will not be beyond the children's achievement level (may appear so at first) if they have learned all of the previous motor skills in this book. You will find young learners enjoy the challenge and faster tempo used for this quick little jig step. To avoid any faulty movements that may be difficult to break, teach jigging without music in the beginning. When music is introduced (practice phrase below) play slowly. Increase the tempo as performance ability improves.

Directions for Jigging. Take the weight off the right leg by resting ball of right foot beside left. On the first count of music after "pick up" touch the right heel forward, quickly jump onto right foot placing the left heel forward at the same time, quickly jump onto left foot placing the right heel forward at the same time. Continue alternating this step till end of music. There are two jig steps to each measure of music.

Building further jig skills. This same jig step can be performed only instead of touching the heel forward touch the toe instead (toe jig). A scissors jig is another form of movement for building finer motor skill. Start with feet together. Jump, landing with feet apart in an open position, jump, landing with feet together in a closed position. Continue this out and in movement till end of music. A more complex form of scissor jigging would be performed crossing the feet when jumping together.

JIG MUSIC

David Laakso

IRISH DANCE

This Irish Dance can be a fun-learning activity for the classroom or a Saint Patrick's Day performance in a school program. Chairs are required in the beginning (kindergarten type) to simplify teaching. Due to space and the need for chairs you may want to work with only half of the class at a time. Once the children have learned to skip in a back circle you can discontinue using chairs if you wish. To begin the dance, place as many chairs as space permits in a straight line about three feet apart with children sitting on the chairs.

Introduction. Children stand placing the ball of the right foot (no weight on it) beside the left foot. Place the backs of hands on hips (4 measures).

STEP ONE

A. Jig step seven times alternating starting with the right foot (3½ measures of music). Rest in place for ½ measure of music.

B. Each child skips eight times around their own chair to the right (4 measures of music). This is the back skipping circle small children find hard to understand unless they have an object to skip around.

C. REPEAT ALL of A and B of Step One (8 measures of music).

A. Side skip four times to the right side (2 measures, weight will end on the right foot). With arms held straight at sides of body, turn to the right once or twice in place on balls of feet (2 measures).

B. Reverse all of A in Step Two side skipping to the left side and turning left (4 measures).

C. REPEAT ALL of A and B in Step Two (8 measures).

STEP THREE

A. REPEAT ALL of Step One (16 measures).   End

IRISH DANCE

David Laakso

Costuming suggestions for this dance on page 52.

STEP - CLOSE - STEP - HOP

There are two practice phrases for learning the combination of step-close-step-hop. For small children it will be easier to understand this combination if it is learned as component parts then combined as a dance step. Step-close-step-hop is the prerequisite for many similar combinations of dance. It is also a basic schottische step.

Step-Close directions. Facing front, step the right foot to the right side (1 count), then step the left foot beside the right foot (1 count). With feet in a closed position rest two counts of music. Continue to step-close with rests seven more times to right side. Reverse this entire step doing eight step-closes to the left side. The rest counts are used in this step so the small child will be able to define a single step-close.

Step - Close

David Laakso

<u>Step-Close-Step-Hop directions</u>. Revue step-hop learned previously in this book before beginning this combination. Then demonstrate to the class how step-close and step-hop is combined to make a dance step (no music).

To step-close-step-hop, you step right foot to right side (1 count), step left foot beside right (count 2), step right foot to right side (count 3), hop on right foot (count 4). Reverse this step doing step-close-step-hop to the left side (4 counts). This step is performed facing forward while moving to each side. Continue alternating this step till end of music.

<u>Building further skills</u>. Step-close-step-hop is the same as a basic schottische step. Select some schottische music with a strong beat and have the children try a schottische dance. It can be performed from side to side (sometimes crossing over rather than closing feet), or progressing forward. To stylize, swing the free foot forward every time you hop. An easy basic combination for a schottische dance is two schottische steps followed by four step-hops.

Step-close-step-kick is very similar to step-close-step-hop. To perform this dance step, eliminate the hop (directions for right side), instead kick with the left foot. Another similar combination is step-close-step-heel. In this dance step the left heel (directions for right side) strikes the floor without taking any weight on it. Like step-close-step-hop these similar dance steps should be practiced by alternating the movement.

Step - Close - Step - Hop

EASTER SONG AND DANCE

This lovely song and dance was created especially for the holiday of Easter. If this dance is used for a school program, children could make their own Easter hats in the classroom and wear them for a stage performance.

Dance directions. Depending on the size of the class, arrange the children in one or two well-spaced lines. Lyrics may be sung before the dance is performed.

Introduction. Dancers are standing in place touching the ball of the foot (no weight on it) beside the left foot. Boys are posed holding the brims of their hats with the right hand, and girls are posed holding their skirts at the sides with both hands. This pose is held for the four measure introduction.

STEP ONE

A. Starting with the right foot, do step-close-step-hop four times alternating (4 measures).

B. Point the right foot forward tapping the floor three times (no weight) keeping the leg straight; then step on the right foot in place (1 measure). Repeat B three more times alternating (3 measures).

STEP TWO

A. REPEAT ALL of Step One (8 measures).

STEP THREE

A. Turn to the right in place taking tiny steps on the balls of feet (1 measure).

B. Kick the right leg forward slightly off of the floor, step the right foot in place. Kick the left leg forward slightly off the floor, step the left foot in place (1 measure).

C. Repeat A and B in Step Three for three more times (8 measures).

STEP FOUR

A. REPEAT ALL of Step One (8 measures).

STEP FIVE

A. Dancers turn to the right running in their own little back circle, (same floor pattern as Irish Dance when skipping around chairs) returning to their original position (2 measures).

B. Step-close to the right side (2 beats), bow forward tilting from the waist (2 beats). Reverse the step-close and bow to the left side (1 measure).

C. Repeat A in Step Five (2 measures). Repeat B only take just one big gracious bow to the right side using two measures of music. End

EASTER SONG and DANCE

Lillian Lindley

Costuming suggestions for this dance on page 57.

wake up in the morn-ing and then hur-ry to get dressed.
world is oh so beau-ti-ful, it's

spring-time at its best. Find the Eas-ter bas-ket

bun-ny's left for you, full of eggs and can-dy

some sur-pris - es too. Step out - side in

your new clothes, you can't help feel-ing fine, we're

thank-ful for so man-y things, we're hap-py all the time.

33

TWO-STEP PRACTICE

The importance of this dance step is that it builds skills for more intricate forms of folk dance. In teaching this dance step, keep in mind it is very similar to galloping. A revue of galloping and an explanation of its similarity to galloping will help the slowed learner.

When a two-step is preceded by a hop, it becomes a polka. The two-step is a very good prerequisite for learning the polka as it not only is similar, but the uneven rhythmic pattern is the same. Children should learn a basic two-step before performing the dance "Roundup Time" which follows.

Two-step directions. In the beginning, children find it easier to perform a two-step if it is learned from side to side rather than progressing forward. A single two-step is performed to one measure of music to a count of 1 & 2.

Step to the right on the right foot (1), quickly slide the left foot up to the right, cutting the right foot off floor (&), step to the right on the right foot (2). At this point, when learning, the child should have his left foot off the floor to be certain weight is on the right foot. To reverse the two-step, step to the left on the left foot (1), quickly slide the right foot up to the left, cutting the left foot off floor (&). step to the left on the left foot taking weight (2).

Use the practice phrase that follows for practicing alternating two-steps.

TWO-STEP PRACTICE

step close step step close step etc.

ROUNDUP TIME

(Western Lariat Dance)

This is a real fun dance for both boys and girls that teaches a basic two-step and a gross hand-eye motor skill. Twirling a lariat makes this song and dance exciting for all ages. Instructions for making a novelty lariat in the classroom are given on page 56. Even the most reluctant boys who refer to dance as "sissy stuff" will respond with enthusiasm when they can perform with a lariat. You'll find even the very youngest of learners can twirl these novelty lariats with skill. If you are using the dance for very young children, see instructions for modifying movement in the dance note.

Information on song and dance. The Western song and dance is in two parts. The dance is performed first (entire class), followed by half the group singing while the other half twirls. This will give ample room for the twirlers to perform and allow the singers to concentrate on the lyrics.

SONG AND DANCE DIRECTIONS

Divide the class into two well-spaced lines. The front line is made up of twirlers who will twirl after they dance; the back line consisting of singers who will sing after they dance. Each twirler holds a lariat in his hand coiled up like a rope when he dances. Interchange groups so all the children will have an opportunity to twirl or sing.

DANCE
(Entire Group)

The song is played once through for the dance.

Introduction. With feet together, bend knees up and down, keeping time to the music (4 measures).

STEP ONE

Starting with the right foot, do eight alternating two-steps (8 measures).

STEP TWO

A. Starting on the right foot, gallop or side-skip three times to the right side (1 & 2 & 3 &), then step on the right foot taking weight (4th count). This uses two measures of music. Do one two-step on the left side and one two-step on the right side (2 measures).

B. Reverse all of Step Two, moving to the left side (4 measures).

LYRICS AND TWIRLING

The entire arrangement is played once through a second time for twirling and singing.

Introduction. On the 4-measure introduction the Twirlers (front line) spread out so they have ample space for twirling. Singers (back line) move back, giving as much space as possible for lariat group.

TWIRLING DIRECTIONS
(Back Line Sings)

First Line of Lyrics. Make figure eights with lariats (4 measures).

Second Line of Lyrics. Make circles with lariats (4 measures). The more skilled students will enjoy side-skipping from side to side at the same time they are making circles with their lariats.

Third Line of Lyrics. Repeat first line (4 measures).

Fourth Line of Lyrics. Repeat second line (4 measures).

Tag Ending. Twirlers drop down on one knee, twirling their lariats completely around their bodies with a fast twirling action.

Note: Very young learners can replace the two-step with side-skipping and turning in place to right or left. Older learners will have the ability to dance and twirl at the same time. For fun and creativity, give children an opportunity to work out their own dance steps and twirling routines.

ROUNDUP TIME

Lyrics by Jeannette Le Captain

David Laakso

In the West at round up time lar-iat's turn a - round and round,

steers are caught from be - hind lar-iat's turn with - out a sound.

In the West at round up time lar-iat's turn a - round and round,

rides are rough cow-boys fine horses buck-ing up and down.

BASIC POLKA

A quick little hop on the "and" count before you do a two-step and you have turned this movement into a basic polka. The transition will be natural if the class has first mastered the two-step. For very young children or slow learners I always use a "see," "hear" and "do" method when first introducing a polka. By "see" I mean showing the class how the hop is added to the two-step. "Hear" is having the class first "talk" the step to the music, such as "hop-step-close-step" using the same rhythmic quality you would use for physical performance. This kind of perceptual input works well with young children as movement becomes more complex and is dependent upon the thinking process. Some children make the mistake of leaping rather than hopping. A hop is springing into the air from one foot and landing on the same foot; a leap is springing into the air from one foot and landing on the opposite foot. It's a difficult habit to break if you don't correct it right away.

Use the first eight measures of "Spacemen's Polka Dance" as a practice phrase for learning a basic polka.

Directions for a basic polka. One polka step takes one measure of music (& 1 & 2). Hop on left foot (&), step on right foot to right side (1), quickly slide left up to right foot (&), step on right foot to right side (2). Reverse this same movement to do a polka step to the left side. Like the two-step, children will find it easier to do a polka step from side to side rather than progressing forward in the beginning.

SPACEMEN'S POLKA DANCE

This dance offers a fun way to begin an exercise on understanding gravity. The children can make a space helmet (page 58), dance a gay polka, and pretend to float around on the moon. The first half of the song is used for doing a polka and the second half of the song is used for pretending to float freely around as spacemen do on the moon.

SPACEMEN'S POLKA DANCE

(Played Once Through)

STEP ONE (first half of song). Arrange class in well-spaced lines.

A.   Starting to the right side, do six polka steps, alternating (6 measures).

B.   Starting on the right foot, do 4 alternating skips, traveling forward (2 measures).

C.   REPEAT ALL of A and B, only travel backwards on the 4 alternating skips (8 measures).

STEP TWO (second half of song). No formation is required on this half. Discuss what it would be like to be able to move without gravity, then allow them to move freely about the room as spacemen do. They will enjoy creating their own interpretations of moonwalks (8 measures).

SPACEMEN'S POLKA

Words by Lillian Lindley
Polka Rhythm

Music by David Laakso

Hop on one, then on two, it's a
dance, to this tune, when you're

fun dance to do. Here on earth you will
up, on the moon, you will see you may

find you can pol - ka eas - i - ly 'cause
be float - ing free - ly all a - round 'cause

gra - vi - ty   is strong. If   you   gra - vi - ty   is gone.

slower

GHOST MASK

Indian Beads

COSTUMING

IDEAS

Pilgrim Boy's Hat

Irish Plug Hat

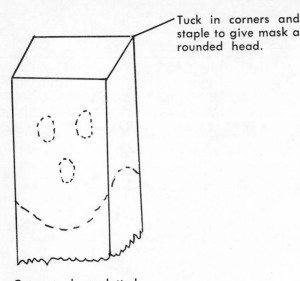

Tuck in corners and staple to give mask a rounded head.

Cut out along dotted lines.

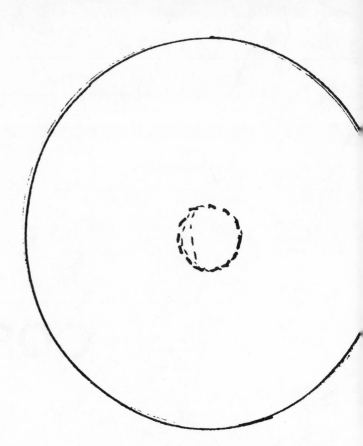

Cut a circle out of an old sheet, about 1½ yards in diameter. Cut out hole for head.

COSTUMING FOR HALLOWEEN GHOST DANCE

The ghost mask is made from a 7″ white paper bag. They can be purchased at your local bakery stores. The bottom of the mask is cut away so the bag will rest on the child's shoulders and yet hide the neck opening on the front of the ghost costume.

The ghost costume is made from an old sheet the children would bring from home. The neck opening should be no larger than necessary to fit over the child's head.

COSTUMING FOR THANKSGIVING DANCE

Make the Indian vests out of large, heavy grocery bags as diagramed. They can be trimmed with cut-outs in colorful construction paper, using various designs and pasting them to the vest. Trim can also be done with crayons or paint. Fringe the bottom edge of the vest with scissors.

The Indian head pieces are made from what is left of the paper bag after the vest has been cut out. Use double thickness on head bands for durability. Stape to fit child's head size. These head pieces can be trimmed in the same manner as the vest. Real feathers can be used or, if not available, make them out of construction paper.

Indian necklaces are made inexpensively by using "bead" size macaroni. Add color to the necklaces by using a few of those multicolored plastic beads found at most toy counters intermittently throughout the string.

Use the instructions for the "Irish Plug Hat" on page 53 to make the boy's Pilgrim hat, only reverse the paper pie plate so the brim of the hat turns down. Make a large buckle from colored construction paper to trim the hat. The hats will be effective made in white to match collars and trimmed with a black buckle.

Pilgrims collars and girls' Pilgrim hats can be made from several materials, preferably in white. Felt is one of the most satisfactory. However, they can be made from oilcloth, plastic, imitation leather, nonfraying material, crepe paper, large-size construction paper or large white paper bags. Ties are made of the same material used in collars and hats, except when using paper. It requires one-half yard of 36″ material to make two collars and one girl's Pilgrim hat.

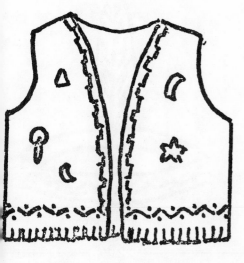

Indian and Chief Vest

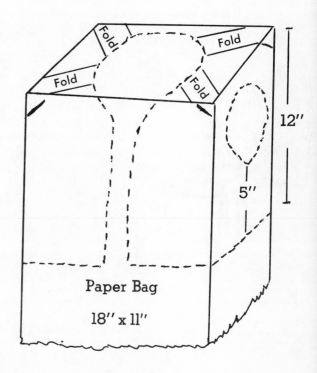

Paper Bag

18″ x 11″

12″

5″

Fold Fold Fold Fold

Cut out vest along dotted lines. Fold in four corners to round shoulders.

Pilgrim Girl's Hat

Pilgrim Boy's Hat

Pilgrim Girl or Boy Collar

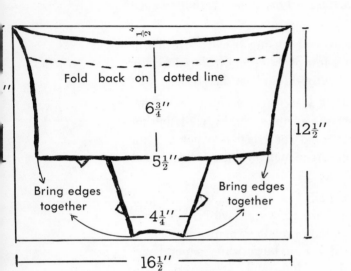

Fold back on dotted line

$6\frac{3}{4}''$

$5\frac{1}{2}''$

$12\frac{1}{2}''$

Bring edges together

Bring edges together

$4\frac{1}{4}''$

$16\frac{1}{2}''$

Pilgrim Girl's Hat Pattern

Bring edges together, matching darts by stapling or sewing. Attach ties.

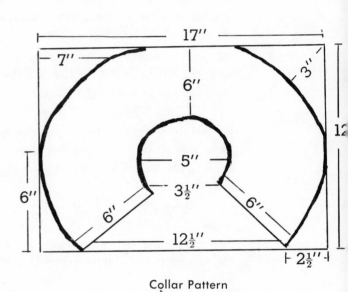

$17''$

$7''$

$3''$

$6''$

12

$6''$

$5''$

$3\frac{1}{2}''$

$6''$

$6''$

$6''$

$12\frac{1}{2}''$

$2\frac{1}{2}''$

Collar Pattern

Attach Ties

Indian Beads

Chief Headpiece

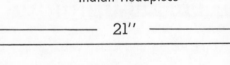

Indian Headpiece

$7''$

$3\frac{1}{2}''$

$1\frac{1}{2}''$

$21''$

Chief's Headband

$21''$

$1\frac{1}{2}''$

Indian Headband

COSTUMING FOR CHRISTMAS TOYSHOP

SOLDIER—Military straps and belt are two inches wide and the length of each is determined by the size of the child. Straps cross in the back the same as the front. Straps should be red and can be made out of any of the following materials: oilcloth, felt, leatherette, or plastic. Staple straps to the belt in their crossed position and leave the opening at the back of the belt for getting in and out.

The military hat is made out of a white gallon plastic bleach jug as diagramed. Cut a visor pattern out of paper and trace onto the upper part of jug. Trim hat with the same material as was used in straps. Hat has a tendency to sit on top of the head, but it is effective this way. Staple an elastic band to the hat to go under the chin to hold the hat on securely.

Boys should wear their own dark trousers and white long-sleeve dress shirts to complete the costume.

DOLLS—The shift-type costume for the dolls is very easy to make. It slips over the child's head and has no zipper or buttons. The only sewing is at the shoulders and sides of dress. If a sewing machine is not available a stapler can be used. This pattern fits an average 6-year-old. Mid-thigh is a good costume length.

Use brown wrapping paper or newspaper to cut out pattern. Be sure paper is first cut to the size as diagramed before drawing costume pattern.

The following materials are suggested for the doll costume so it will have a full-bodied look. Use red oilcloth, felt, plastic, or lightweight leather-ette. A firm cotton material can be used if cut with pinking shears. The pattern doesn't allow for any hemming of raw edges.

The doll bonnet hat is made out of half a paper pie plate. The plates with fluted or rippled edges are the best choice for hats. These plates are sold in various pastel colors, of which green would be a good choice for Christmas. Cut hat out as diagramed and staple ties to fasten under the chin out of the same material as the costume.

MAKEUP

Face makeup for stage performance can give a real toy look to the children. It can be done by outlining the eyes and making eyelash lines with an eyebrow pencil. Lipstick can be used for making cupid lips and blotchy cheeks.

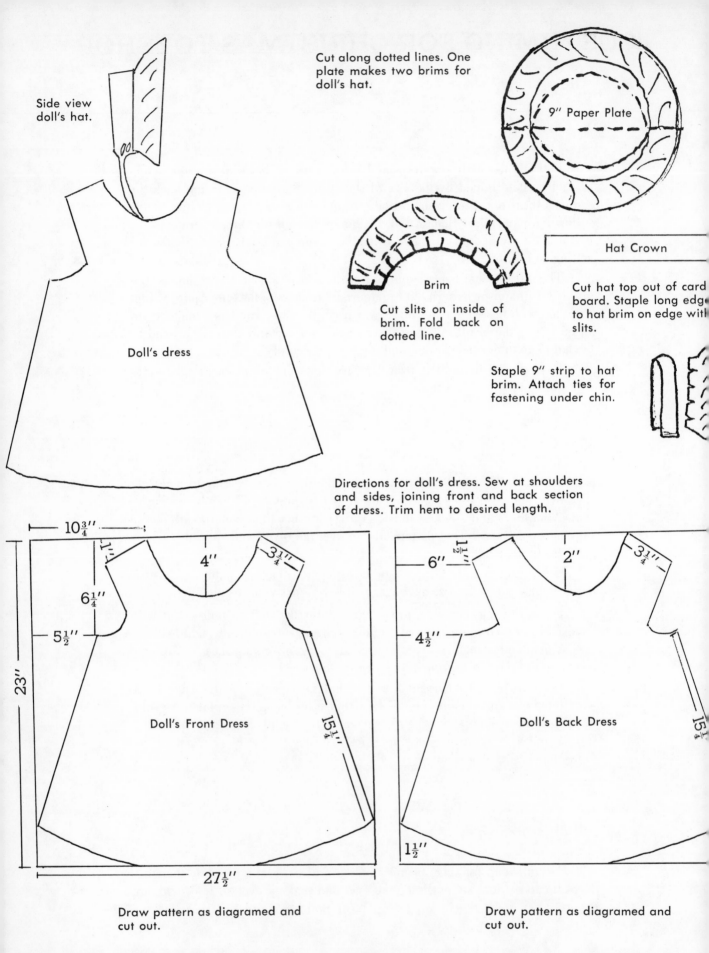

Side view
doll's hat.

Cut along dotted lines. One
plate makes two brims for
doll's hat.

9" Paper Plate

Brim

Cut slits on inside of
brim. Fold back on
dotted line.

Hat Crown

Cut hat top out of card
board. Staple long edge
to hat brim on edge with
slits.

Staple 9" strip to hat
brim. Attach ties for
fastening under chin.

Doll's dress

Directions for doll's dress. Sew at shoulders
and sides, joining front and back section
of dress. Trim hem to desired length.

10¾"

4"

3¼"

6¼"

5½"

23"

Doll's Front Dress

15¼"

27½"

6"

1½"

2"

3¼"

4½"

Doll's Back Dress

15¼"

1½"

Draw pattern as diagramed and
cut out.

Draw pattern as diagramed and
cut out.

Soldier Hat

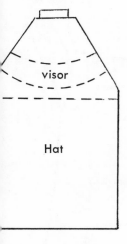

Hat

visor

Cut visor and hat along dotted lines.

Soldier Straps—Belt fastens in back. Cut strips of material 2" wide for belt and straps. Length depends on the size of the child. Overlap at belt back and fasten. Straps are stapled to belt as diagramed.

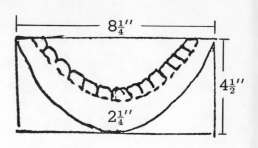

$8\frac{1}{4}''$

$4\frac{1}{2}''$

$2\frac{1}{4}''$

Make paper visor pattern. Plastic visor will be cut from jug top. Cut slits on plastic visor and fold along dotted line. Staple to hat.

COSTUMING FOR EDGAR AND THE COPYCATS

To make this physical activity something special and exciting, let the children make their own costuming in the classroom. You will need only one snowman, which is made of corrugated cardboard, tissues, black construction paper and a small amount of material. The snowman costume can be a group activity for the whole classroom. Each child can make his own winter hat and scarf from crepe paper and a small piece of yarn or string.

WINTER HAT AND SCARF FOR COPYCATS

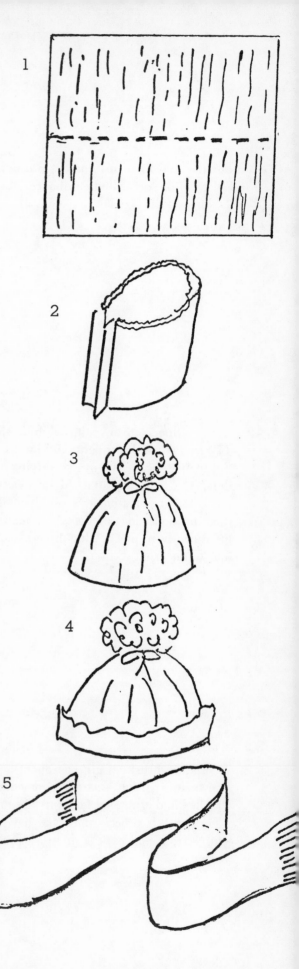

1. Cut a 22″ by 20″ piece of crepe paper and fold in half along dotted lines. You can make five hats out of a standard-size package of crepe paper (10 feet long and 20 inches wide).

2. Bring both ends together and staple to form the crown of the hat. Turn right side out so stapled seam is on the inside of the hat.

3. Gather the top of the hat together and tie with a piece of string or yarn. Separate the cut edges on the top of the hat and flare to give a pompom effect.

4. Fold the bottom edge of the hat up about 1½″, flaring slightly to make a rolled edge on the hat.

5. Cut a 40″ by 6⅔″ piece of crepe paper and fringe both ends to make a winter scarf. One standard package of crepe paper will make exactly nine scarves (10′ by 20″).

1. For the snowman costume cut two ovals (17″ by 20″) out of corrugated cardboard. Make two slits 2″ long as diagramed.

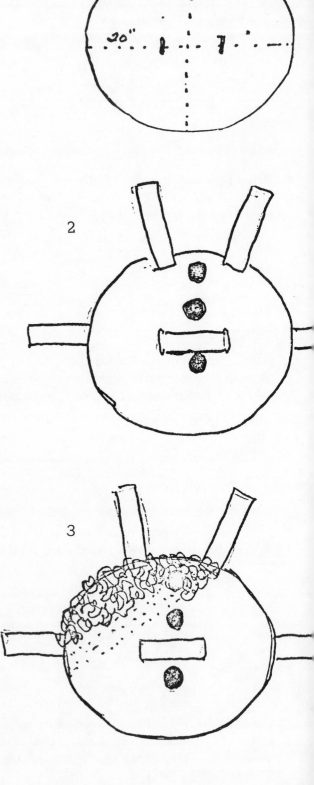

2. Using white cloth or felt, cut four shoulder ties 17″ by 20″ and two belts 18″ by 2″. Attach two ties to the tops of both ovals for tying on the shoulders. The belts are attached by weaving through the slits. This belting ties snugly under the costume on both sides of the waist, holding the costume firmly in place. Glue three black paper buttons to the front section.

3. Spread or brush on glue on about a third of the snowman's front section. Immediately apply crushed and crumpled facial tissues to glued area. Continue this process until you have covered the entire front and back section (except buttons) of costume.

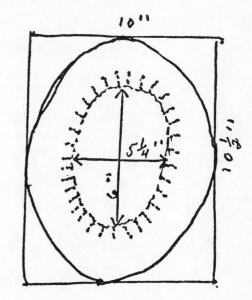

4

10"

10½"

5¼"

3"

4. Snowman's top hat is made from lightweight cardboard. Cut out brim and center of brim along dotted lines, making slits. Fold the tabs up.

5. Cut out crown section. Bring ends A and B together and staple to complete the crown section. Staple or glue crown to brim. Paint top hat black.

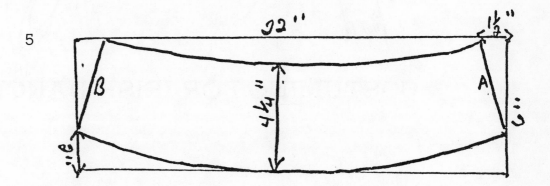

5

22"

1½"

4½"

B

A

3"

3"

COSTUMING FOR IRISH DANCE

These costume ideas are very easy to make and are effective enough to fill the need for the children to use in a school program. If the children are not doing this dance for a public performance, the miniature Irish plug hat will be a good project for the art class. For a performance the boy would wear his own white shirt with a green bow tie. Shorts should be a dark color worn with white knee socks. The girl wears a weskit over her own dress which should be more or less styled with a gathered waist and puff sleeves for a peasant look.

IRISH PLUG HAT

The brim of the hat is made from a green 9″ fluted paper plate. Cut the center of the plate away, making slits so the crown can be attached as diagramed. The top of the hat is made from a 2-lb. cottage cheese container. Staple the container to the plate as pictured, forming the hat. Masking tape is another method of attaching these two pieces together. The outside of the crown (cottage cheese container) is covered with green construction paper using the pattern on the diagram and trimmed with a shamrock. The crown of the hat can also be made with cardboard if cottage cheese containers are not available. To make the hat in this manner, use the same pattern for "crown covering" only add ½″ on each end to allow for overlap in the back of the hat. String or hat elastic should be stapled on hat to stay firmly on head.

WESKIT AND BOW TIE

The girl's weskit can be made of green felt, oilcloth, plastic, or other similar material. Cut out waistband and straps according to directions on diagram. The straps can be sewed or stapled in place. Lace the front of weskit with narrow ribbon. The boy's green bow tie can be made out of crepe paper, felt, or other materials.

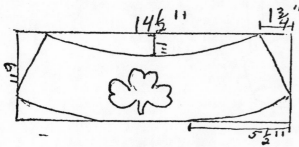

Cut out covering for crown of hat. Draw shamrock for trim and glue to cottage cheese container.

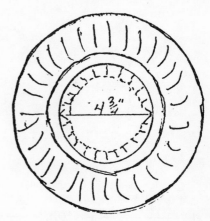

9″ Paper Plate

Trace inside circle using top rim of cottage cheese container for a pattern. Cut out center of plate along dotted line. Cut slits and fold up.

2-lb. cottage cheese container

Staple to plate to form crown for hat.

Irish Plug Hat

Boys' Bow Tie

Girls' Weskit

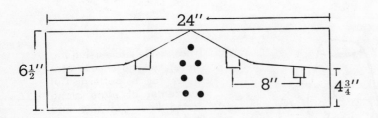

Weskit Waistband. Punch out holes for lacing.

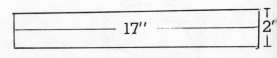

Weskit Strap. Attach straps 2½" from center front and 1½" from center back. Insert laces and tie at top.

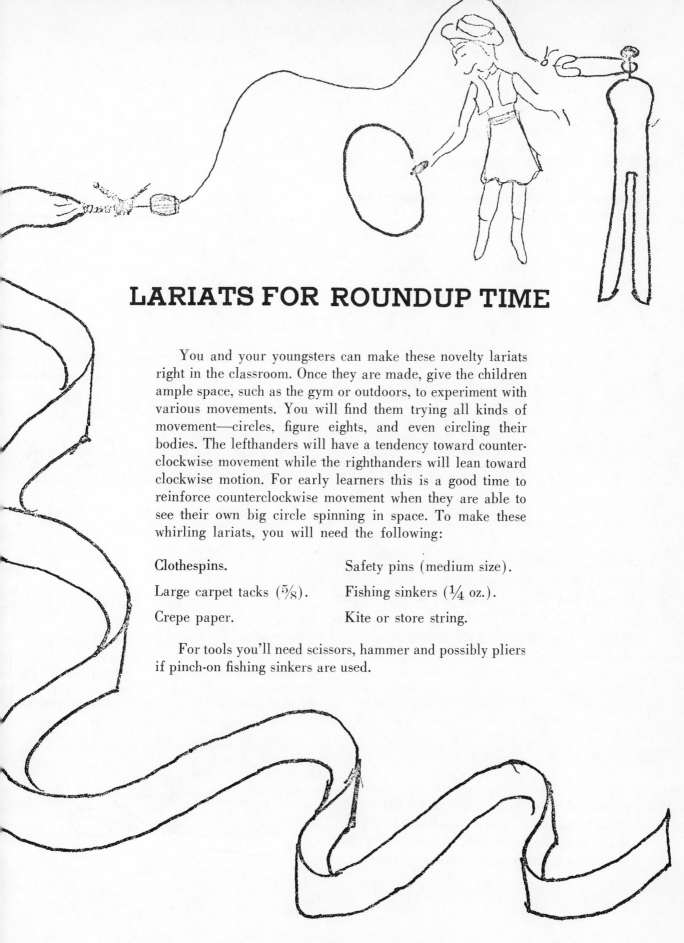

LARIATS FOR ROUNDUP TIME

You and your youngsters can make these novelty lariats right in the classroom. Once they are made, give the children ample space, such as the gym or outdoors, to experiment with various movements. You will find them trying all kinds of movement—circles, figure eights, and even circling their bodies. The lefthanders will have a tendency toward counterclockwise movement while the righthanders will lean toward clockwise motion. For early learners this is a good time to reinforce counterclockwise movement when they are able to see their own big circle spinning in space. To make these whirling lariats, you will need the following:

Clothespins.	Safety pins (medium size).
Large carpet tacks (⅝).	Fishing sinkers (¼ oz.).
Crepe paper.	Kite or store string.

For tools you'll need scissors, hammer and possibly pliers if pinch-on fishing sinkers are used.

1. Without unfolding your package of crepe paper, cut a ¾″ strip for each lariat ribbon. A standard-size package of crepe paper will make ribbons ten feet long.

2. Stretch and twist a few inches on one end of your lariat ribbon to form a twisted cord. This end will be used for tying.

3. Attach a safety pin (on eyelet end) to the top of your clothespin with a large carpet tack. Do not hammer tack all the way into clothespin as safety pin must be able to move freely. Tie a 27″ string to the head of your safety pin.

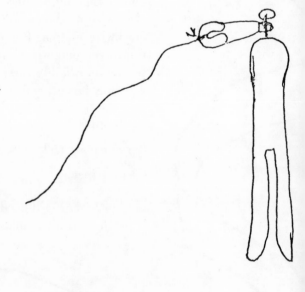

4. Tie the other end of the string to the twisted end of the lariat ribbon. Put a fishing sinker (¼ oz.) on the string next to the knot. You need the weight of the fishing sinker to make the lariat turn.

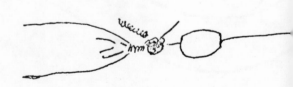

EASTER HATS FOR BOYS AND GIRLS

These hats can be worn for a performance in a school program combined with their own dressy clothes or can be used as an Easter art project.

The girls' and boys' hats are made with the same pattern as diagramed. The crown of the hat is made from a plastic gallon bleach jug which comes in many pretty colors, and the brim is made from cardboard. Use construction paper or paint to cover the brim to match the bleach jug crown. Yellow is the most effective color to use for boys as it gives a straw hat look. The hat is trimmed with a hatband made from construction or crepe paper, ribbon, plastic, or other materials. The girl can use any color and trim with nylon net, flowers, feathers, or other materials. Hat elastic or string should be stapled on the hat to tie under the chin.

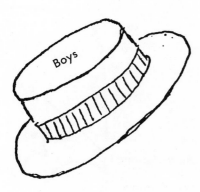

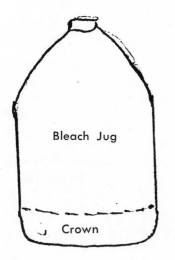

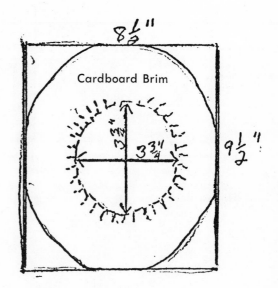

Cut 2″ bottom off jug to make crown.

Cut out brim and center of brim along dotted lines and make slits. Fold slits up and staple to crown.

SPACE HELMET

Your Spacemen's Dance will take on new meaning and interest when children can make their own space hats. Boys are especially fond of this project, and if encouraged, will have a lively class discussion going on spacemen's clothing and equipment. Each child could bring his own plastic gallon jug from home and make his own, or just a few could be made for classroom dramatization. For this space helmet you will need:

1 plastic gallon jug.

8½" by 11" piece of heavy paper or light cardboard.

2 brass fasteners.

1 ft. piece of rope or thick yarn (optional).

If the helmet is used for stage use, spray with silver paint. Frame for face shield is effective in black.

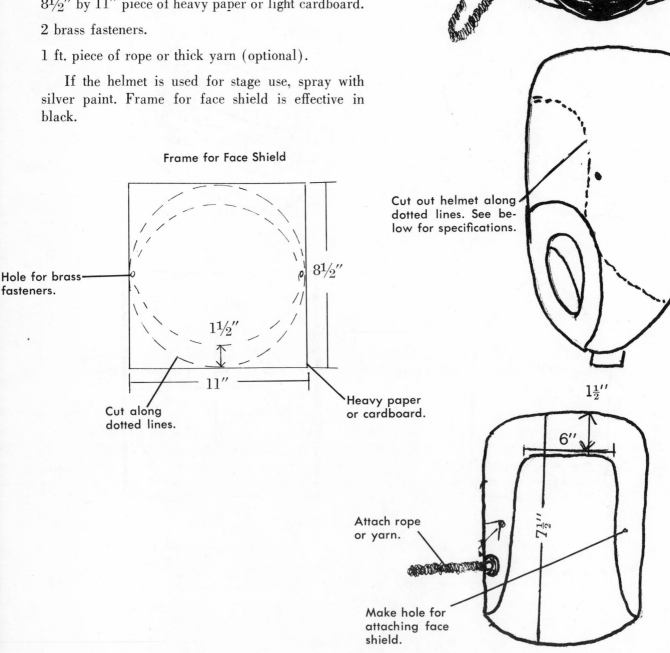

Frame for Face Shield

Hole for brass fasteners.

8½"

1½"

11"

Cut along dotted lines.

Heavy paper or cardboard.

Cut out helmet along dotted lines. See below for specifications.

1½"

6"

7½"

Attach rope or yarn.

Make hole for attaching face shield.

Recordings are available for all activities in this book.
Send $4.50 (three 45-rpm records) for complete recordings.

LECAPTAIN PRODUCTIONS
P. O. Box 199
Escanaba, Michigan 49829